15-WAYS TO AVOID DYSFUNCTIONAL REAL ESTATE DEALS THAT WILL COST YOU MONEY

By WILLIAM HAWTHORN

By William H. Hawthorn PUBLISHER:

Erika Brooks - Phone: 919.447.3305

Email: ebrooks@lulu.com and pr@lulu.com!

The "typical" result one can expect to achieve is nothing. The "typical" person never gets to the end of this book. The "typical" person fails to implement anything. Thus they earn nothing. Zero. No income. Perhaps even a loss of income. "Typical" people do nothing and therefore they achieve nothing.

Be atypical. Do something. Implement something. If it doesn't work, make a change...and implement that. Try again...try harder. Persist. Then reap the rewards.

Dedication

To my wife Pamela and two kids Jessie-Rae and Emma-Lee whom help me and support me often. No matter how crazy my ideas is!

Contents

Introduction

I have always wanted to go into real estate investing but everyone I met kept telling me I would not make it. They told me it was a hard world and some got frustrated and ended their financial lives. I didn't believe, of course. Do you believe the same? If you do, you better hold this book closer to your eyes or simply drop it down this moment. For those like me who didn't believe, cheers to you, I am going to help, so now let's get busy. This book is for those who want to know how I was able to make it.

I didn't believe, because why would I disreguard what I saw others do because I couldn't make it? I tried to get my first deal and I almost considered quiting myself, several times. No joke, I mean, it was not easy; I could have lost the seller and the house I bought, plus lose everything I had at the time. I was depressed for twelve hours. Just twelve hours because, I knew I had people to prove wrong. Afterwards, I went for several trainings and I learned some things which I'm going to share with you in this book.

You are not in the freaking real estate business if you're not making offers "lesson" is what changed my life. Whatever you're doing other than making offers is

1

just a joke in this unbelieveable industry. You cannot buy a house until you make an offer, it is just impossible. You can inherit a house, but you can't buy a house unless you make an offer.

When I got into the business it was different than it is now because of the Internet; back in the day it wasn't as easy as it is now because we had to do everything manually, like free recorded messages, mail, signs, figuring out what houses were worth, etc.

I was taught that when you first start, the average person needs to make about 15 offers to buy a house. That's nose-to-nose ... toe-to-toe with the seller. Not some MLS (Multiple Listing Service) offer. I am talking about at the sellers kitchen table or on their coach in their living room. Personally, I averaged about five offers to buy a house, but I made thousands of offers and bought hundreds of houses as of the writing of this book.

How long will it take you to make 15 offers a week? A month? Three months? A year? Three years? Five years? Ten years?

"Oh my Gosh, all I could think of was how to get through those 14 offers. How quick can I get through these 14 so I could get to the 15th?" I constantly wondered. That was how I got started.

However, I made shyty offers. I did stupid stuff by

just grinding through those 14. It was all I was doing, but nobody hated me. Nobody was mean to me (well maybe once in a while, but only when I asked for it). They let me look at their house. They let me make them offers. There was nothing wrong with what I was doing. In fact, most were grateful I was so honest and trying to help them.

Now let's get down to me teaching you …

Where To Find Motivated Sellers

Making deals with realtors and bankers can be rather tough. I remember one time my partner didn't want to use a proof of funds letter, so I wrote a check for the house I was making an offer on and gave it to the realtor as my "proof of funds." I told him, "Here's the check of $60,000 for this house in Waterbury Connecitcut. Negotiate the check then call my lawyer and he'll do the title work with you."

Three hours later, what do you think the realtor did? He called me back and said, "The bank doesn't do that. We can't accept your offer."

This was another life changing moment for me. I realized then I was in an insane world. Yes, this world is crazy. I figured out that there's nothing better than communicating and making an offer to a motivated seller. I learned to do my marketing and let sellers get to me through the marketing filters I could set up. By the time they got to me, the marketing would filter the "suspects" out so I would have less work to putting a deal together. For example, my free recorded message is almost six minutes long. Who would listen to a six-minute message? A "prospect!"

You should know that some may hang up. But if

they dial six on my little system and go to my live operator, the operator would ask them a few questions and then send the responses from the call to me. Or it goes to my acquisition manager and then to me. There's my arrogance peeking it's head out; I just hope you get how my little system saved me TONS of time. I hope you get it because after you make a lot of offers, you'll realize that what I'm teaching you, not a lot of people know it.

The seller is privileged to have somebody like me or you sit in their living room helping them with their problem because if they could just put it on the market and sell it for what we can give them, they would have.

At the end of the day, what you're doing is you're matching your plans with your sellers' plan or a lot of times the seller doesn't have a plan, so you help them figure out a plan.

You're looking for somebody that is willing to accept your plan or you align with what they want to do with this house and improve their life. Like for example: Harold the seller, has his wife on him, he's got to… she wants another… He can't do it because the house is holding them back. Our plans match because guess what, I want a house with those problems, right, because I can fix them. So I tell Harold I will take the house with the problems.

What happens is when you make offers, you're

actually building a case like you're in court. It is like you have a jury that is juring you so you have to make your case. If you were a lawyer and you had to go into a courtroom in front of this jury and plead your case, would you be prepared? I know my answer ... yes. Then you should do the same with your offers. You should have an idea or a theory based on what your case should be.

We do some testing with them to see if our plan matches thiers. We talk to them on an opening call. We talk to them on a closing call. We went through a process that allowed us to get a picture of what financial and mental situation the seller is in and where he/she wants to go. You build your case as they give you information, you keep looking at these and keep plugging them in and moving them around and keep building them until all of a sudden, you get a perfect theory to win your case.

Once you know the math of the deal, you're ready to move on because you are not going to make an offer with just math. You're dealing with a Homosapien Being which means they have feelings and they have a bunch of other crazy stuff too and you have to satisfy that portion of it. Think of it this way. When you talk mathematically with them, you're talking to their analytical conscious mind. You have to go through the subconscious mind, where all the touchy-feely stuff is. That is where you're going to make your deal, not with the math. They're going to close, when they feel warm and fuzzy because you did a good job with both.

At the end of the day, I feel like my job is to extract as much information and start building my case with these little building blocks as if it were a brick wall and when I'm all done, I've gotten enough information I've surrounded the seller and I with this wall and I can now organize the information and help them do the right thing for them.

If you get it right now and learn my stuff, you'll have the same experience as I do because I'm going to show it to you. You're going to have the experience to be able to help that seller get their information organized and do the best thing for them. Sometimes it is you buying their house, sometimes it is not. It is a numbers game for you because you should not expect to buy every house you're sitting in. Just get through the numbers. If you help 14 people, what do you think is going to happen on number 15? Somewhere, somehow somebody is going to say yes, or tell somebody and you're going to end up with a deal you can earn money doing.

15-Rules To Avoid Dysfunctional Deals & Help You Protect Your Money

Number One

As discussed earlier, deal with motivated sellers which means they're chasing you and you're not chasing them. If you're chasing your buyer (when buying a house) or your seller (when selling a house) on a deal, then they're not fully satisfied. They should be chasing you. And when I mean chasing you, if you don't call them in day or two, they call and say, "Hey, what's going on?" This is a very good indicator that you have a motivated seller and that you should keep your attention on that deal because you're going to buy that house (or sell it) as long as the math makes sense.

In the past, I used to do a lot of networking meetings, but now it is once or twice a week. I would go for BNI groups and meetup groups (from http://meetup.com) I would go around and meet people. This is a great place to find attorneys, accountants, painters and contractors. It is also a great way to build a dream team.

One of the things that I hate the most is when one of my networking group members come up to me and say, "Hey, I got someone that wants to sell their house" can you talk to them? I hate those because the way my system works is I put my marketing out and they chase me. This type of lead (the networking guy is giving me) is not the type of lead I like to work with. I believe if you put enough marketing out, if you do lot's of outflow, something will come back. It is the universal law. I don't want to chase anybody not ready for me, and I don't want to be chased like I'm playing hard to get either. Just know if they are not motivated and continuously trying to stay in the deal then I really don't want to deal with them.

So I found that "motivated" means you are helping them with something no one else can help them with. And money is only one (and truly not the most important sometimes) of all the ingredience that makes the deal a success. And once you master this skill, you are WAY ahead of everyone else "flipping houses" in your town, county, or state. You will stand out like a beacon of light in the denses fog ever.

Number Two

Know that sellers are paying you a shyt ton of equity to solve their problems. Not only that, but these problems are their unsolvable problems. He is wlling to pay to have you relieve him of it. If I buy the house from our example seller Harold for $80,000 and it is worth $100,000, how much equity did he pay me to solve his problem? $20,000, right? So, I better know what his problem is, don't you think? If the seller is paying $20,000 me to fix his problem, I better know what it is.

I may not know how to solve the problem, which is where "Newbie Investor's" make their biggest mistake, because they think you need to know how to solve all their problems. Well, I got news for you. I didn't become me by knowing everything; I became me because I just had big balls and I just went and did it. So, when Harold said to me, "blah, blah, blah, blah, blah," I'm like, you know what, Harold, "I never did anything like that, but I'm going to go figure it out. Will you sell me the house if I figure it out?"

Then I would scurry around and figure out how I can solve the problem. I can tell you right now that when I talk to my money guy, my lawyer and my mentor, that I'm very specific with what Harold wants me to do. But I don't have to promise him anything until I am ready. I can just say, "Hey Harold, I have never done this before, but you know what? I got a mentor. I got a lawyer. I've got resources. I'll figure it out."

You better know what that problem is because he's going to pay you $20,000 to fix it. Of course, once you know what the problem is, you have got to help him get rid of it or resolve the problem or you won't stay in the deal.

Also if think you know what the problem is and you checked the problem buy repeating it to Harold before you storm off and go to work, then you say to Harold, "You told me that you can't sell this house because you can't pay the monthly payments. If I fixed it, will you sell me the house?"

If he says, "No, that's not why I'm selling a house, that's not true. No, I'm selling the house because I want to get divorced," then you know you're dead wrong and you need to find out why the house is stoping him from getting divorced? Otherwise, you will never buy the house. He isn't getting a benneft he wants at the closing table and will not show up.

So always check the problem. Don't think you have it figured out. Always repeat it back to the seller as soon as you see it to make sure he says, "Yes, that's my problem." So that you both are on the same page then solving the problem becomes the journey you both will take..

Number Three

Never ever buy a house without equity in it. There's only one exception to this rule. When you do a Slot (Sandwich Lease Option Transfer) Deal, where you are buying an over-leveraged house and you create the equity (To learn more about this go to:

http://flippinghousesforrookies.com/freestuff).

Otherwise you need to make sure the day you close on any house (and when I mean close on that house, or sign Lease Option paperwork, or you get the deed), you must have equity (or profit). Do not close unless you have equity or you can create equity that day before the sun sets. It is that simple.

If you do what I do, you should know how to do the paperwork because each one of these deals has its own set of paperwork. If you understand how to do the paperwork and you know what the equity is, it just meshes together. Now you know how to solve Harold's problem, get to work.

Number Four

If you have no or low capital or don't want to risk your capital, stay in the pretty house business. This means doing Terms Deals and not putting up large sums of money for ugly houses. Ugly houses are the hardest, most dangerous, and most risky way to buy and sell houses. Why would you want to put a mortgage in your name? Why would you want to have insurance, since if that house burns down, you're responsible? Why do you have to deal with the contractors along with it? Because there's a lot of crap that goes along with it to make $24,000 (by the way, national, average, $24,000 a deal). Now you might think $24,000 is a lot of money. But then how long have we been doing that rehab for? Peter The Rookie (my Podcast buddy @

http://flippinghousesforrookies.com/podcast) told me 10 months to do our last rehab.

10 months because we've been getting jerked around by contractors. It was not Peter's fault. Rather it was my fault because I let it happen.

I have a student who is in my private coaching for six months, bought, rehabbed and sold a house and made a years salary while being a stay at home mom. She met me in a meet-up, bought my $500 course, found at: http://flippinghousesforrookies.com).

Within a month, she had two houses bought. The first house she bought was a $90K renovation, she flipped it 4.5 months later and earned $85,000 net money. A month and a half later, she closed on her second house for a $43,000 profit.

The third house she got was hit by a storm burst that a tornado went through. A $430,000 house. She paid $203,000 for it. They put $79,000 into it. She hasn't even finished the house and wrote a contract on it for $430,000 and she just put another contract on another new purchase. None of it is her money. She did not having any contractors when she started. She did not know how to do it before we started. She's an exception. She's a hustler. All I'm saying is that you pick which one on my 7-buying strageies you'll get good at, you can do the same.

Go here to watch an interview with her live:

https://goo.gl/ycvFjo

If you have no or low capital and you don't want to risk your capital, stay in the pretty house business.

This means doing Terms Deals and not putting large sums of money on ugly houses. If you work in the pretty house business and do lease options (or rent-to-own) deals. So if things get bad and you need to walk, you have a seller that's pissed off at you, but that's it. You won't lose $180,000 because you signed personally for the loan and ended up in court or have a bunch of contractors put liens on your house or on a house that you have got to give up. Stay in the pretty house business. At least get going in the pretty house business and when you find the ugly houses and you're ready do it, but don't start there unless you have some experience.

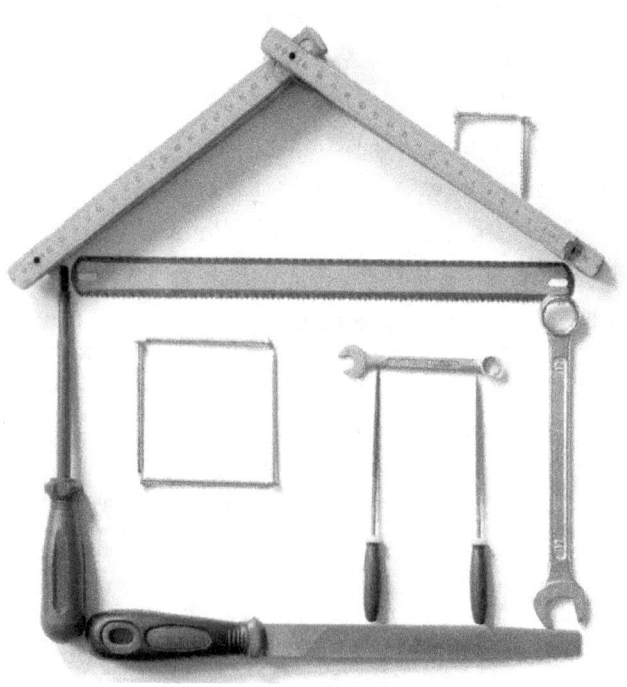

Number Five

Do not use your credit or a bank loan to buy property. This sounds weird, doesn't it? You're better off using hard and private money. The simple reason is that hard and private money are asset lenders. They lend the money on the property, so they lend money up to 70% of what the property is worth once fixed up hoping that you default then they take their 70% and turn it into a 100% if you don't pay and they have to take the house back. Most of them are flippers or old time flippers, they realize there's fast money in flipping and they have no problem with taking the house back because they owned it at 65 or 70 cents on a dollar. So, they're lending on the house, not on your performance to pay.

If you're dealing with a hard money lender that's asking you for a deposit of $10,000 or $20,000 and they're pulling your credit, they are a banker in disguise. They are in a masquerade party and they got their mask on. Don't deal with them. If you can stay away from them, stay away.

The point that I'm trying to make here is that these guys are credit based lenders and you should use asset lenders. There is so much money to buy real estate, and you know where you find that money? It is hidden right underneath your nose. It is in IRAs and 401Ks. They can't be touched for 10 or 20 years (in most cases), but if you do it correctly, you can buy real estate with it.

Number Six

D o not make promises you cannot keep. Do not write checks you cannot cash. Like I would say to Harold, "Well Harold, I don't know how to solve your problem, but I'd like to go find out how. If I come back with a solution, will you sell me the house?" That's a promise. I didn't have to promise him, yes, I'm going to buy the house. I'm just going to tell him the truth and explain I need to figure it out. Done this way you don't have to be an expert right off the bat. You can learn as you go.

I have got a private coaching group, and we meet every Monday night by phone. The biggest reason why people hire me as a coach is because first of all I'm real as shit and second of all, when you're in my coaching program and you're doing a deal, I stick to you like glue and act like the safety net so you don't have to worry about going too far "to figure out" what Harold has going on.

I always believe in giving a minimum of three offers in a house so the seller can choose. See the seller is not used to having choices. So if the sellers choses to sell for $120,000 and wants to close in 30 days. My coaching client doesn't have to worry about producing the $120,000 in 30 days because I am there to help him.

Then I make sure that my coaching client has the paperwork and can perform. I'm not your partner, but I act like one. I make sure that you're not going to fall down and get hurt; this is what I offer in my coaching program.

Only make promises that you can keep. If you can't keep them, then find somebody like me who can help you keep them.

For more information about my group, go here:

http://flippinghousesforrookies.com/advancedcoaching

If you want to make a million bucks, go find a guy that has a million bucks. You want to know how to sell a house or buy a house, go find a guy that sells houses or buys houses and ask them, "How do I do this?"

Number Seven

D o not have tunnel vision. I did this with a house a few weeks ago. I walked into a condo, thinking the guy only wanted cash which he was asking $98,000. It didn't need much renovation as it was already livable. Just a little dated, but livable. I was thinking that I would give the guy $65,000 to $70,000, if he pushed me I would entertain $73,000.

This is a simple offer because the ARV (After Renovated Value – or fixed up number) was $100,00. So the formula is:

ARV times 70% minus repairs = MAO (Maximum Allowable Offer).

So I start like this:

"What would have to happen for me to buy your house today?" I asked.

"I don't want to give you a number and start bidding against myself," he said.

"Just give me your number and I'll tell you yes or no," I pushed.

"$85,000," was his response.

I had tunnel vision and didn't think it through. We

left minutes after that. I was in the car with David, my acquisition manager at the time, and he asked, "Why would you do that? You could get $1200 a month. His payments were only $700 a month. It had $500 a month positive cash flow, there's a college right next door. You can rent that thing like crazy. Why don't you invest $85,000 to make $1200 a month or in this case, $500 a month?"

"You know if that was a Subject to Deal (go to http://flippinghousesforrookies.com/freestuff for an explinataion of "subject to deals) it could be bought at 80% on the dollar. If he said that he had a mortgage for $80,000, you'd want to take over the mortgage payment." I said "you know David, your right." I had tunnel vision and lost the deal.

We tried to resurrect the deal, but is was too late. He found someone else to buy. Because it was a good deal. And those type of deals don't hang around long!

7-figure invetor's know these are the most important things to know about a deal:

a) What do they owe?

b) How much their payments are?

c) Do you think they're motivated?

This is very basic stuff to know. Reason is because too many times I have had people interpret what they think the guy wants to do and then they get into the house and they get tunnel vision and they blow a deal. I would rather go in there with my mind open and get my building blocks (pieces of data) and do my thing and build an offer. It is not straight information or injected opinions when talking to the seller. You should do the same.

When you go in, do not have a narrow, viewpoint, right? This means you're not flexible.

Virginia's learning how to buy and sell houses. I teach her how to do "Subject To" deals but she has a consideration that she would never sell anybody a house and put the deed in their name and keep the mortgage in her name.

She would never do that. "This is stupid, this is crazy" she says. "Why would anybody do that?" Well, she just blocked herself off from a bunch of deals because she thinks that nobody will do so. So, who do you think she's going to attract?

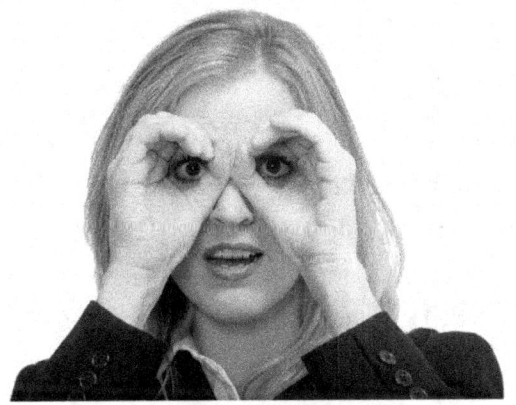

Number Eight

Be honest. Think that's too simple? Let me explain. The realtors can't take it when I explain the cost to sell to a seller before they sign a listing contract. Realtor's do it at the end; when it's too late! And in about 98% of the cases it is WAY lower than expected, and the seller is not happy. Be honest. What you need to do is create a comfortable environment for your seller. If you want to be a seven-figure earner in real estate, this is exactly where the rubber hits the road. When you learn how to do this one thing, you will crush it.

You have to make it comfortable for them to communicate to you, so they are honest with you.

If you're honest with them, they're honest with you. I just talked about this on my coaching call the other night. So, you start texting somebody, right? This opens up a conversation. Next, you're on the phone with them doing an opening call, discussing what the seller is willing to do.

Then you move into the closing call which is more like, "Well, we buy houses like yours alot. Here's how it works. You give me the deed and the mortgage stays in your name. What do you think, will that keep you awake at night?" "Oh, it will, how about if we do a

Lease Option?" Then, "How about I come out and check out the house to make sure the house qualifies first, and then we'll talk about how it all works?" All we're doing is making an appointment.

You get to the house, you walk around the house, you look at the house, and make sure that everything's good. Are you with me so far?

You sit down in the living room, their living room, not yours. They're on the couch, you're on the couch. What do you do? This was the question I asked the other night in my private coaching group. This is where you make millions of dollars.

Right at that one spot. Usually at this point I have some idea of what their situation is. So, what I do is I start with a story. Now, it might be my story; I have got a lot of stories because I have been doing this for a long time. I either tell my story or a story about my friend or something I read. By doing this, I make it comfortable for them.

You have to break that social veneer, cut it right in half and get them to talk to you so you can really help them.

They have to feel like you're sincere and they have to drop their guard. You need to make it a safe environment for them to communicate. You cannot evaluate. You cannot judge them. You just have to flow with it. And if you don't do that, you will lose deals. Clear?

Did I get too passionate about this? I have tried to do seminars on this, but nobody shows up. For the first time two months ago, I had one or two people buy tickets because most people don't think that it is important. But this is the most important part of the deal.

You make all your money on that couch talking to your seller. And collect it once you sell. So you better be damn good on that couch when talking to the seller, make sense?

The words you use in life are directly proportional to what you have in life!!

Number Nine

Deposit money. I'm going to emphasize this because for two years I've been saying, "No money down, no money down". Other gurus you go to, 'no money down' to them is less than $5,000. I think it should be less than $2,000. I don't think it should be anything, if you can help it. There's only one reason why a person asks for a deposit on a house. Do you know what that is?

The only reason why somebody asked for a deposit on a house is because you provoked them to ask. If you don't bring it up, they won't bring it up. Like Fatima (my coaching client) said, "If they're asking for a deposit, that means being honest was done wrong by you. Because they don't trust you, they want money security. They'll ask for a deposit because they don't trust you."

If you put money into a deal, get the deed in your name because that's the only way to protect your investment. Done this way, your money stays in your control. If you put up $3,000 in a deal that you don't have a deed for, you are risking your capital?

You don't go into a Lease Option Deal and say, "Oh yes, I will clean the place up. We'll take all the garbage out of here. Yes, we'll do all this stuff." The next thing you know, you have spent $5,000 on a house you don't own.

If you want to do that, here's what I suggest. Pick a neighbor in your neighborhood and go over and renovate their house for them because it is the same damn thing. Go to your neighbor's house and say, "Hey, we're going to take all the garbage out of your house and we're going to cut the grass. We're going to spend $6,000. What do you think?" Because that is what it is like when you're putting money into a Lease Option house.

If you do not have the deed in your name, don't spend money. Even if you have a lot of money it doesn't matter, know that your money is at risk. Don't come whining to me that you lost $5,000 or more.

Number Ten

I f you don't know how to do rehabs, don't go look for rehabs. If you don't have money and you don't have good credit and you can't go to a hard money lender and play by his rules, don't market for that house.

Don't have such a scarcity mentality that you're going to take any deal that comes along. You're going to beg, borrow, and steal to do it only to find out it's a 90-day wonder. You know what a 90-day wonder is? You buy a house and in 90 days you think: "Why the hell did I buy it?"

I had a lot of those because I was pushing myself, "I got to buy a house. I got to buy a house..." "My wife's giving me a hard time because I spent $10,000 on a credit card for real estate training and I got to pay that $10,000 back because she's really pissed off at me because I bought..."

Some of your best deals are no deals. Use the math, do the study. Learn, spend your Saturday morning or Friday night or whenever you can to go through these materials a dozen times so you get it. If you don't know how to rehab, don't do rehabs. By the way, this also means do not do wholesale either. That is tougher that rehabbing, I promise!

Number Eleven

Very important to know, make offers only after you know the equity the seller has and not on what they're asking. They can't control what they owe. They're not going to change the taxes. They're not going to change the mortgage company. They're not going to change the loan, so if they owe $150,000, they owe $150,000. Figure out how you're going to pay it, whether it is monthly until you can find your buyer or you're going to pay cash and get rid of it, but figure it out.

What you're going to negotiate is the equity. So, you need to figure out what is the equity (or the sellers profit).

Just in case you're curious, we have a form, a one-page form that does this for you and the customer. It is called the Cost to Sell Worksheet. When they are done with filling it out, it tells the seller exactly how much their equity is and it tells you exactly how to negotiate with them.

Once you know what the equity is, use one of my seven ways to buy real estate, found at

http://flippinghousesforrookies.com/freestuff)

so you can figure out how you're going to pay them.

So, I say to Jim the seller, "Jim, you've got a mortgage of $150,000 and the payment is $1000 a month and the you want $20,000 walking money, how about the mortgage stays in your name, and the deed goes in my name" I promise to pay him his $1000 a month. If he wants $20,000, I will tell him, "Jim, I'm going to write a note for $20,000. No interest, no payments. When I sell the house, I'll pay you the $20,000."

If he says, "Oh no, I need cash now."

Then I say, "How much cash do you need Jim?"

"I need five grand."

Okay, no problem. I double the number he is asking for and subtract it form the selling price, "If you want five grand, I can only pay $160,000." I take the $5,000, I double it, make it $10,000, subtract it from the $170.000 he asked for and I make an offer of $160,000. Do you get it?

So now he's got a decision to make. Do I want the $5,000 now and take less, or do I just want to wait for the $20,000? How important is that five grand?

I can only do this when I'm making an offer on the profit of the equity. I have to structure the deal around the equity, not the asking price. Most people will say, "Oh, you're selling for $200,000. Why are you selling for 200,000?"

They either overestimated or underestimated, they don't ever do it right. So why not get to the heartbeat of this creature and do it right the first time? Say, "When you close on this house, what were you expecting to walk away with?"

They're going to tell you exactly what to offer them. "Well, I want $10,000." If you can give them $10,000, they'll sell you the house.

If you asked the right questions, you don't have to make an offer. What you have got to do is take the information, start organizing it and know when to pop that question and then they tell you exactly what to do.

Because they feel comfortable. They know you're honest. Hey have confidenc. They know you know what you're talking about. You organized the whole thing so they can think, "Oh, that's what I want." And it just goes whoop.

By the way, all that I'm talking about pertains to pretty houses. When you're buying ugly houses, you don't need to know any of this stuff. It goes like this: I'll give you a $10,000. That's it. I'll give you a $30,000. That's it. You don't need to do all this fancy talking with ugly houses. But when you're buying pretty houses, you're looking for terms. You have got to know all this stuff.

Number Twelve

Use my Seven Offer Strategy. This came about because I sat in too many houses were my one or two offer ideas didn't work. So I would leave with my tail between my legs; without a deal. So I started learning more and getting clever. And was doing realy well with it. Then I hired my first Acquisition Manager and had to explain it all to him. That's when I came up with the LTV (Loan To Value) ratio I use to this day.

See, if you divide the amount owed into the amount being asked (or your going to pay) you will come up with a percentage.

Let me give you an example: You owe $70,000, and the house is worth $100,000. You type $70,000 into your calculater, hit the divide button, then type in $100,000, then hit the equals sign and you will have your LTV number.

See, it doesn't make sense to make a Wholesale offer of $55,000 if he owes $70,000, right? It just makes the seller mad and harder to deal with on the second offer.

Before 2009, you want to know what my biggest problem was? Credit cards was my biggest problem.

You want to know why? People went out and bought all kinds of crap which by the way was all over the house and in the yard. They would refinance to cash out the credit cards, and then they would get blank credit cards and they would do it again.

Now they're completely in debt and asking me to give him the third or fourth or fifth profit. They suck the money out of the house and blew it and now they're asking me to give him another profit.

Everytime they took money out of the house, it was profit. Including the profit they want from me now. This was a problem for a long time. Nowadays it is not so bad because 2009 readjusted this, but for a while it was a big problem.

So if you know what they owe you can be smarter about your offers. Now you can adapt one of my seven strategies on how you can pay them the money they owe, plus their profit.

My saying is: "I will pay whatever you want for a house, as long as I get to pick the terms."

Knowing my 7-Deal strategies will increase your percentages to buy a lot.

To see the exact math and a few videos on this, go to: http://flippinghousesforrookies.com/freestuff

Number Thirteen

Number Thirteen is a simple formula. Once you know what the seller is willing to except, now you have to make a decision on if you want to buy.

Here's how you evaluate a deal. Money now, money monthly, money later. When you fill out my Prospects Suspect form, it takes the entire deal and puts it on one piece of paper so you can evaluate it. You can go get that at:

http://flippinghousesforrookies.com/freestuff.

It is just one piece of paper. It has everything you need to know about that deal on one piece of paper. When you look at that paper and start wondering what you're going to do, you ask yourself, "Where's the money now? Where's the money monthly? Where's the money later?"

Please pay attention to me. When you have just one of these in the deal, like "Money now" you do not spend a shyt ton of time on this deal because you're only making $3,000 or $5,000; you're not going to spend six months on this deal, like if you're going to do a Getting the Deed Deal where you got $10,000 for a deposit, you got $400 a month positive cash flow you make different decisions.

I just did a deal last month where I bought a $260,000 house; I paid $110,000 for it and borrowed $125,000 from a private lender and he used funds from his IRA. This allowed me to get five years to pay for it with monthly interest payments.

The house needed $50,000 worth of work because it was dated. I spent about $8000 cleaning it up. I sold it for a $220,000 on a Lease Option. The guy gave me $10,000 down. I have a $1000 a month positive cash flow, and I have $90,000 in the back end.

Was that worth spending time on? Yes. Why? Because I'm making a lot more money. Time is money. If I'm going to do a Slot (Sandwich Lease Opting Transfer) Deal, I'm only going to make five grand. I am not going to want to spend much time on this deal, make sense?

If you cannot get terms from your seller, you can get terms from your lender if you use IRA money.

The only rule to this is that you need to use the Rehab Retail formula, which is where you're going to buy 70 cents on a dollar minus repairs.

So, I paid $110,000 knowing that if my buyer goes in there and he completely wrecks the house, I don't care because I was going to spend $50,000 on it and I have that money in the deal so anytime I want I borrow $50,000 and fix the house.

In other words, I've got nothing to lose and everything to gain. Instead of asking the seller to give me terms, I went and got my private lender to give me terms and I bought on a Cash Deal. Then I sold it on a Lease Option. I kind of used two or three different kinds of ways to buy from my seven. This is what I refer to as hybrid deal.

Number Fourteen

Give no attention or resources to anyone trying to sabotage you or your deal. This is a Ben Settle thing. Ben is a copywriter that I absolutely adore. I buy everything he has. I read everything he has. I just love the guy. Ben Settle said, "Why nourish and make strong a rabid dog that's trying to maul you?" So, if you have somebody who's trying to blow your deal up, do not give it attention because if you give something attention, it solidifies and happens.

If you have a lawyer who blows your deal up, what you do is move on; you ignore that dirty, rotten SOB and you keep going with your seller until the seller just doesn't want to go anymore.

Do not put attention on who's going to blow up your deal or make your deal harder; just keep working through it until you can get your seller to see your point of view, because if you're being honest and you're being straight and you really are trying to help them, you could bring them through it. So, don't feed the rabid dog that is trying to maul you.

Only respect people that respect you. In this business there is a lot of disrespect, especially with realtors. If they don't respect you and what you can do, don't respect them. Don't be mean. Don't be abusive. Just tune them out. They don't deserve your attention or your resources.

Have your standards. Who you're going to give your attention? Who are you going to help? What resources are you going to use? Who are you going to assist? I dealt with someone who owned a house worth $100,000 once. She owned it free and clear and then ended up with a $17,000 tax bill. I told her point blank, "I'm not your buyer".

"Why not?" she asked.

"Because I don't want to rob you of your house, if you're trying to solve a $17,000 tax bill. How about I turn you onto my resources? We get you a mortgage that will only be a few hundred dollars a month and we pay the taxes off and you keep your house?"

I respected her because she was very nice. She let me into her house; she did everything I asked her to do, so I paid back. Now, we did this for about three weeks and she got frustrated; she had kid problems and I ended up buying the house for like $35,000. But that was because I respected her. She would not sell that house to anybody else except me because I tried to help her. She respected me, I respected her and my standard was I should try to help her. So, I gave her my resources. I gave her my attention. I gave her what I could to help her.

Number Fifteen

D on't put anyone, like your attorney, your seller, your closing agent (anybody) on a pedestal. People looking at $800,000 houses put the seller on a pedestal because of their money staus. You know what happens when you do this? They look down on you. You lose your power. You lose your mission. You lose any respect. You lose a lot.

Don't put your attorney (or closing agent) on the pedestal as well. Don't call up your attorney and be like, "What do you think I should do?"

"No, it's more like this. I'm going to do this. What's my liability?" That is how you talk to your attorney.

You don't go to your accountant and say, "You think I should?"

No. Say, "If I do this, what's my tax ramification?" Don't put them on a pedestal. Mind your own business. Take care of yourself. Ask the right questions. Don't put them on a pedestal because they will look down on you and you lose respect.

This business has a lot of 'know it alls'. A lot of people want to tell you what to do and try to sell you their shyt. They want you to get into a coaching program. They want this, they want that. Respect yourself, know that this is a real honest to good business. The pretty house business and creative financing is such an amazing business.

Conclusion

Y ou may have encountered some mis-spelled words or bad grammer, maybe some of my Connecticut accent in this book.

But if you can forgive that and hear what I tell you, it will help.

Why?

Because I have done millions and millions of dollars in real estate, and I am willing to share it with you.

I am not a proessional author, or a professional website guy, for that fact an attorney. But I am one kick-ass deal maker.

And I want to make it so you don't get "bogged-down" with too much stuff and don't get started. But instead I want you to feel safe with what I am telling you so you can go out and try it.

When it works like I have explained it, you will soon begin to trust me.

Definition of trust buy the way: When your words match your actions. People will trust you.

Also, one of my biggest barriers to helping folks is this … I explain how I have done something many,

many times. Without much variation in results.

I explain it to you. It doesn't work out the way I explained. You think I did something wrong. Or what I am teaching is not correct. So you end up with bad results and blame me.

But in fact have never given the consideration that you may have misunderstood (and in most cases don't even know it) what I was teaching you.

My philosophy is don't memerise things hoping to pass a test (like in school) but instead understand the subjet by observing it. And using it.

For example: I teach someone how to fix a car. His test should be … here is a broken car, now make it run correctly.

And the best lessons in the world are going to come from your mistakes. All I am tring to do is show you where to expect these mistakes so you are prepared for them when they come. You WILL NEVER do it perfectly. Every deal is different.

As a teacher my obligation is to make sure the student understood by applying.

I strongly suggest if you are the type of person who deosn't read much, or feels you have to see something to learn, or you read and can't apply, even worse, you read and get to the end of a page and don't remember what you read, you should go get this AMAZING BOOK:

Author: Sean Clouden

Title: The Power Of Words

You can find it on Amazon. Or wherever you buy books now.

To reach Bill Hawthorn for questions, go to:

http://flippinghousesforrookies.com/support

For LOT's of FREE stuff, go to:

http://flippinghousesforrookies.com/freestuff

To listen to our podcast's, go to:

http://flippinghousesforrookies.com